Three Things God Finds Impossible To Do

RON BARNES

Southern California Seminary Press
El Cajon, California

Three Things God Finds Impossible To Do

©2016 Ron Barnes

Published by Southern California Seminary Press
El Cajon, CA

ISBN: 9780986442-1-0

The illustration on page 12. Adapted from Bridge to Life © 1969, The Navigators. Used by permission of The Navigators. All rights reserved.

Unless otherwise noted, all Scripture quotations are from The Holy Bible, New King James Version (NKJV), copyright © by Thomas Nelson, 1984.

DEDICATION

This book is dedicated to Dr. Doug Bray who taught me that Jesus is too wonderful to keep to myself..

CONTENTS

1   Is There Anything Impossible For God?   1

2   God Finds It Impossible To Love Us With A Greater Love   3

3   God Finds It Impossible To Give Us A Greater Gift   6

4   God Finds It Impossible To Offer Us A Better Deal   9

5   Conclusion   16

    Questions for Personal or Group Study   19

    Bibliography   21

CONTENTS

1

IS THERE ANYTHING IMPOSSIBLE FOR GOD?

He cannot…

- Lie—His Word is truth (John 17:17)
- Die—He is immortal (1 Timothy 1:17)
- Deny Himself—He is faithful (2 Timothy 2:12)
- Have a beginning—He is eternal (Hebrews 1:8)
- Be defeated—He is King (Revelation 19:16)
- Change—He is immutable (Hebrews 13:8)
- Swear by anyone greater than Himself—He is the Most High (Hebrews 6:13)
- Be ignorant—He is all-knowing (Isaiah 46:10)
- Be successfully tempted by evil—He is righteous (James 1:13)

And, John 3:16 infers three more things that God finds impossible to do.[1] The context of John 3:16 is a conversation between Jesus and Nicodemus, a highly respected teacher of the Old Testament. Nicodemus had a physical birthday, but no spiritual birthday. So Jesus tells him how to be born into God's family.

In John 3:14-16, Jesus says, "Just as Moses lifted up the serpent in the wilderness,[2] so the Son of Man must be lifted up, that whoever believes in

---

[1] This general idea was first heard by the author during a course at Dallas Theological Seminary taught by Dr. Larry Moyer, Founder and CEO of Evantell (evantell.org.).

Him may have eternal life. For (here's why the promise of verse 15 is true) God so loved the world that He gave His only begotten Son, that whoever believes in Him should not perish, but have eternal life." So then, based upon John 3:16, what three things does God find impossible to do?

---

[2] This story is found in the Old Testament book of Numbers 21:4-9.

2

GOD FINDS IT IMPOSSIBLE TO LOVE US
WITH A GREATER LOVE

Our Maker's glorious love has been lavished upon us in a certain manner. The word "so"—"God so loved"—points to the way in which God loves us. Let's savor three mannerisms of God's great love.

First, God loves us intensely. The Greek term for "loved" ("For God so loved"), in this context, describes an intense love, regardless of the object of that love. John 3:16 portrays God's intense love for the world.

When my daughter, Allison, was little, I would sometimes say to her as I tucked her in for the night, "Did you know, Allison, that God is absolutely crazy about you?" She would smile and say, "I know Dad. You always tell me that." Once I put a note in my daughter Rachel's lunch sack that said, "Dear Rachel, I want you to know that I turn cartwheels of joy over you. I love you very much. Signed, God." I tell my youngest daughter, Hannah, "You are a dream of God."

During their Thanksgiving dinner, a family shared what they were thankful for. When it came to four-year old Joshua's turn, he said, "I'm thankful that Jesus loves me so well." So very young, and yet Joshua understood the truth of John 3:16 that God loves us intensely.

Then second, God loves us unconditionally. The Bible says, "For God so loved the world." Who is "the world," in this context? All people, of all time. And what are we like? Nothing but God-insulting sinners who love to wallow in the muck and mire of shame. Romans 1:29-31 paints our ugly portrait: "They have become filled with every kind of wickedness, evil, greed, and depravity. They are full of envy, murder, strife, deceit, and malice. They are gossips, slanderers, God-haters, insolent, arrogant and boastful; they invent ways of doing evil; they disobey their parents; they are senseless, faithless, heartless, ruthless" (NIV).

But God loves us just the same, because by His very nature, "God is love" (1 Jn. 4:8). As Philip Yancey writes, "Paul—'the chief of sinners' he once called himself—knew beyond doubt that God loves people because of who God is, not because of who we are."[3] Paul also wrote, "God demonstrates His own love toward us, in that while we were yet sinners, Christ died for us" (Rom. 5:8). The One who knows us best loves us most!

During the American Revolution, the outspoken Tory, Michael Whitman, persecuted Pastor Peter Miller anyway he could. But when Whitman was charged with treason and sentenced to die, Miller walked seventy miles to Philadelphia to plead for his life. "No, Peter," said General George Washington, "I cannot grant the life of your friend." "My friend?" Miller exclaimed, "He's my worst enemy!" "That puts the matter in a different light," replied Washington. "I will grant your pardon, Mr. Whitman." Peter Miller took Michael Whitman back home to Pennsylvania, no longer an enemy, but a friend.[4]

Born with a sin nature, we are all natural enemies of God. This is proven by our disobedience to God's Word. But the Good News is, "If while we were enemies of God, we were reconciled to God through the death of His Son, how much more shall we saved by His life?" (Rom. 5:10). There is nothing we can do to make God love us more, or less. He loves us unconditionally—and He never changes (Mal. 3:6).

A third mannerism of God's great love is that He loves us personally. "For God so loved the world that He gave His only begotten Son, that whoever believes in Him should not perish, but have eternal life." English Puritan Pastor, Richard Baxter, once said, "If God said there was mercy for Richard Baxter, I am so vile a sinner, that I would have thought he meant some other Richard Baxter; but when he says, 'whoever,' I know that includes me, the worst of all Richard Baxters."[5]

Jesus said, "Whoever drinks the water I give him will never thirst" (Jn. 4:14). And the Bible ends with God's gracious invitation, "And let the one who is thirsty come; let the one who wishes take the water of life without cost" (Rev. 22:17b). [6]

---

[3] Philip Yancey, What's so Amazing About Grace? (Grand Rapids: Zondervan, 1997), 67.

[4] Craig Brian Larson, ed., *Illustrations for Preaching & Teaching: From Leadership Journal* (Grand Rapids: Baker, 1993), 142.

[5] Elon Foster, *New Cyclopedia of Illustrations: Adapted to Christian Teaching: Embracing Mythology, Analogies Legends, Parables, Emblems, Metaphors, Similes, Allegories, Proverbs; Classic, Historic, and Religious Anecdotes, etc.* (New York: W. C. Palmer, 1870), 752.

[6] God's all-satisfying gift of eternal life can be genuinely offered to all sinners

Someone has said that the love of God is like the entire Amazon River flowing down to water just one daisy, and you are that daisy. God finds it impossible to love us with a greater love. But, there is a second thing God finds impossible to do.

---

because God desires that all be saved (1 Tim. 2:4; 2 Pet. 3:9). This desire led to Jesus offering Himself as the Sin-bearer for all (Isa. 53:6; Heb. 2:9; 1 Jn. 2:1-2). And His death for all provides the only basis for God's command that the good news of Jesus' death and resurrection be proclaimed to all (Acts 1:8). This being true, the offer can be personal to all: "*let the one who wishes* take the water of life without cost" (Rev. 22:17). So, the angel told the shepherds, "I bring *you* good news of great joy which will be for *all the people*; for today in the city of David there has been born for *you* a Savior, who is Christ the Lord" (Lk. 2:10-11). And Paul instructed the Corinthians, "Christ died for *our* sins…and was raised on the third day…" (1 Cor. 15:3-4). The words "*our sins*" includes Paul and the unbelievers to whom he preached (past tense) before they trusted in Christ as their Savior. Paul also charged the individual jailor in Philippi, "*You* trust in the Lord Jesus, and *you* shall be saved" (Acts 16:31a). This personal offer assumes that a personal offering was made by Jesus for the jailor's sins. Of course, Scripture teaches that many will reject God's personal offer of eternal life and on that basis be forever condemned (Matt. 23:37-38; Jn. 3:16-18; Rev. 20:11-15).

3

GOD FINDS IT IMPOSSIBLE TO GIVE US A GREATER GIFT

Out of His great love comes His great gift. "For God so loved the world that *He gave His only begotten Son,* that whoever believes in Him should not perish, but have eternal life." God's glorious gift to sinners is the gift of His own Son, the Lovely Lord Jesus Christ. Imagine the joy-filled fellowship of God the Father, God the Son, and God the Holy Spirit for all eternity past; and the decree is that God the Son will be the Love Gift of the Triune God to earth's God-hating rebels.

"For God so loved the world that *He gave His only begotten Son.*" With Paul we say, "Thanks be to God for His indescribable gift!" (2 Cor. 9:15). Jesus was, and is, fully God and fully Man (Col. 2:9; 1 Tim. 2:5), which makes Him the greatest gift to all people. For, He had to be fully God to be a sinless sacrifice for our sins, but He had to be fully Man to die. But many do not believe that Jesus is God in a body. And John 3:16 is a verse they use to make their case.

"Jesus is not God-in-flesh," they say. "He is *begotten*! He was created by God the Father." Yet, the Greek term for "begotten" is *"monogenes,"* which means one and only, unique, one of a kind. There is no one like Jesus who said, "If you have seen Me, you have seen the Father" (Jn. 14:8-9). No one else has revealed God in human form. He was conceived "of the Holy Spirit" (Matt. 1:20), born of a virgin (Matt. 1:18-25) and lived a sinless life as God in a human body (1 Pet. 2:22).

As a member of the Eternal Godhead, He's in a class by Himself, as God-in-flesh (Jn. 1:14). The word "begotten" does not mean that Jesus was created, but that He is one of a kind. But many also claim that the word

"Son" ("only begotten Son") means that Jesus was the created offspring of God. The word 'son' can mean male offspring. But the same Greek term can also refer to one's character.

For example, James and John were called "sons of thunder," which obviously does not mean that they were the offspring of thunder! Rather, characteristically, James and John were thunderous men, denoting perhaps their fiery personalities.

As applied to Jesus, the word "Son" shows that He is, characteristically, God. "He is the radiance of His [God's] glory, and the exact representation of His nature" (Heb. 1:3). As well, since unbelievers opposed Jesus' claim to be equal with God *because* He called Himself the "Son of God" (Jn. 10:31-39), this proves that the term "Son" is a divine title. And Jesus never denied this claim, which led to His crucifixion on the charge of blasphemy.

Of course, in not denying this claim and being willing to die for it makes Him either (1) a liar—and willing to die for a lie, (2) a lunatic, or, (3) He truly was, *and is*, the Lord of Lords, God-in-a-body. If He is not the latter, we cannot simply call him a 'good teacher,' as many do. If He was a liar, a lunatic—or both—and not Lord, then He was anything but a *good* teacher. And if a liar, or a lunatic, He could not be God, or Savior!

Yes, God *gave* His one-of-a-kind Son to rebellious sinners. On the cross, Jesus absorbed several hours of God's fierce wrath upon sin so that we wouldn't have to endure it forever in Hell. On that brutal cross He suffered:

> limitless pain, cycles of twisting, joint-rending cramps, struggling to breathe. He experienced searing pain as tissue was torn from his lacerated back as he moved up and down against the rough timber.
>
> Then another agony began: a deep, crushing pain in the chest as the pericardium slowly filled with serum and began to compress the heart. At this point it was nearly over—His compressed heart struggled to pump heavy, thick, blood into the tissues. His tortured lungs made a frantic effort to gasp in small gulps of air. Now He could feel the chill of death creeping through His tissues. Finally he could allow His body to die. All this the Bible records with the simple words, 'And they crucified Him.'[7]

Oh, that we might often meditate on the cross, where the glory of God's love blazes so brightly. "For God so loved the world that *He gave His only Son*." Again we say, "Thanks be to God for His indescribable gift!" (2 Cor. 9:15). From **A** to **Z** Jesus is:

Almighty God (Isa. 9:6), the **B**read of Life (Jn. 6:35), **C**reator (Jn. 1:3),

---

[7] Larson, ed., *Illustrations for Preaching & Teaching*, 50-51; and see Luke 23:33.

the **D**oor to Eternal Life (Jn. 10:9), **E**ternal (Heb. 1:8), **F**aithful (Rev. 3:14), the **G**ood Shepherd (Jn. 10:11), the **H**oly One (Mk. 1:24), **I** AM (Jn. 8:58), **J**ust (Isa. 9:7), **K**ING OF KINGS and **L**ORD OF LORDS (Rev. 19:16), **M**essiah (Matt. 16:16), **N**ear to the broken-hearted (Psa. 34:18), the **O**ne and **O**nly Son of God (Jn. 3:16), the **P**rince of Peace (Isa. 9:6), **Q**uick to forgive (Mk. 2:1-12), the **R**edeemer (Eph. 1:7), the **S**avior (Lk. 2:10-11), the **T**eacher (Jn. 13:13), **U**nchanging (Heb. 13:8), the **V**ictorious Warrior (Rev. 3:21), the **W**ay, the Truth and the Life (Jn. 14:6), e**X**cellent (Psa. 8:1), the **Y**es (the "Amen") to all God's promises (2 Cor. 1:20), and **Z**ealous for the salvation of every person (Lk. 19:10; 1 Tim. 2:4; Rev. 22:17).

Hallelujah! What a Savior! He was crucified, and then raised bodily from the grave three days later to become the source of eternal life to all who trust in Him.

So then, God finds it impossible to love us with a greater love, He finds it impossible to give us a greater gift; and there is one more thing God finds impossible to do.

4

GOD FINDS IT IMPOSSIBLE TO OFFER US A BETTER DEAL

"For God so loved the world that He gave His only begotten Son, that whoever believes in Him should not perish, but have eternal life." To wrath-deserving sinners, the stunning grace of our Creator offers us *eternal life*!

What is the condition for having eternal life?

"For God so loved the world that He gave His only begotten Son, that whoever *believes* in Him should not perish, but have eternal life."

But, what does it mean to believe in Jesus? The word "believe" is the Greek term *"pisteuo."* I taught my daughters the meaning of this word by having them stand in front of me, with their backs to me, their eyes closed, and then free fall backwards into my trustworthy arms.

The word "believe" means "trust, reliance," just as you trust in a chair to keep you from falling to the floor and in the doctor to do your surgery correctly. John never uses the term "repentance" in his Gospel because repentance is wrapped up inside of trust. As Jesus said, "Repent and believe in the gospel" (Mk. 1:15). And Paul spoke of "repentance toward God and faith in our Lord Jesus Christ" (Acts 20:21).

For example, in repentance, a person changes his mind about (1) *who* God is as Creator and Savior (Acts 17:22-34); (2) his *sinfulness before God* and need of a Savior (Matt. 3:1-11; Acts 19:4); (3) *who* Jesus is—He is God and man's only Savior (Acts 2:36-38; 4:12; 10:43); and (4) the *inability of human works* to erase his sins (Heb. 6:1).[8] The context of a given Scripture reveals what a person must change his mind about.

Believing in Jesus Christ is also equated with turning to God as the sole object of one's trust (Acts 14:15, 23, 27; 15:7, 19). So then, repentance and turning to God are wrapped up in believing (trusting) in His Son, Jesus, for eternal life. As Jesus clearly summarizes, "everyone who beholds the Son and believes in Him will have eternal life; and I Myself will raise Him up on the last day" (Jn. 6:40).

A student wrote me a note that said, "In junior high I prayed the sinner's prayer, *asking Jesus to come into my heart*,[9] but now I realize I was trusting in saying the "sinner's prayer" instead of trusting in *Jesus* as my Savior. I am now trusting in Jesus alone as my Savior." "Whoever believes in Him," the Bible says, "should not perish, but have eternal life." The words "in Him" rule out any other object of trust for eternal life. Jesus said, "I am the Way, the Truth, and the Life. No one comes to the Father except through Me" (Jn. 14:6).

What is contrasted with eternal life?

"Whoever believes in Him should not *perish*, but have eternal life." The word "perish" stands in contrast to "eternal life," showing that to perish does *not* mean annihilation, ceasing to exist; rather it means the total loss of well-being, *eternally*. To perish is to be cut off from any measure of quality of life, separated from God and, therefore, from *all that is good*. Furthermore, the term "perish" means to be ruined, that is, never becoming the person God wanted you to become, stuck with your boring, miserable, wicked, self forever. And all of your sinful passions and appetites never satisfied.

Beyond this general description of the term, to perish, according to Scripture, begins with the unbeliever being consigned to a literal place called Hades, immediately after he has died. According to Luke 16:19-31, Hades entails at least the following:

- being all alone
- continual bodily agony caused by extreme pain from literal flames

---

[8] Repentance does not mean to turn from sinful practices. A non-Christian does not have the power of the indwelling Spirit to do so (Rom. 8:5-13). As well, turning from sin requires works on our part. Salvation is not by works (Eph. 2:8-9). Rather, an actual turning from sinful behavior (and not merely a willingness to obey God) is the "fruit of repentance" (e.g., Lk. 3:8-14).

[9] Asking Jesus into one's heart is not technically a biblical idea. Jesus comes to indwell the life (heart) of the one who trusts in Him as God and Savior as a *consequence* of salvation, not as a *condition* for salvation (Col. 1:27). The concept of "asking Jesus into your heart" may come from Rev. 3:20, which, in reality, is Jesus' invitation to lukewarm (useless, fruitless) Christians in Laodicea to restore intimate friendship with Him (see context).

- endless thirst for even a drop of water, but no relief from anywhere
- a haunting memory of one's earthly life attended by a stabbing fear that family members may also end up in this place of torment—unless they trust in Christ before they die—but never knowing if they have
- cut off from even one act of God's mercy
- the gnawing regret that you rejected God's plan to save you from eternal judgment
- no joy

Hell, the final location of the unsaved, like Hades, is a person's worst nightmare come true, a horrifying existence of wishing you could die but being unable to die. Hell brings a continuous weeping and gnashing of teeth, if for no other reason, because of the endless sadness and terrifying confinement to extreme darkness (Matt. 8:12). But that's not all! Those in Hell are tormented forever as objects of God's white, hot fury (Rev. 14:9-11). Jesus described the length of Hell and Heaven with the same Greek word, so Hell lasts as long as Heaven! To summarize the ancient words of Dante, if a sign hangs over Hell's entrance it may very well read, "Abandon hope, all ye who enter here."[10]

So, why is the punishment of the unsaved so severe and intolerable? Because every person in Hell has committed the ultimate insult, believing that God is unworthy of loving and worshiping. Hell is so awful because God is so Awesome. Hell is so brutal because God is so Beautiful. Hell is so hideous because God is so Holy. Hell is so severe because God is so Sacred!

The only proper punishment for the rejection of such an infinitely Glorious Being is an infinitely horrifying existence. Anything less would cheapen the infinite worth of God. Hell exposes, at the same time, the depths of the sinner's depravity as a God-hater, and the glory of God's perfect justice leveled against sinners who reject His offer of salvation through Jesus. So then, *Hell shows both the gravity of Sin and the glory of the Savior!*

What is the character of eternal life?

The word "life" is a noun and the adjective "eternal" assigns an attribute to this life. By nature, it is eternal, and therefore cannot be lost—once saved, always saved. Our good works for God after we are saved (1) are the fruit of the Holy Spirit's control of us (Gal. 5:22-23), (2) are the natural expression of our ocean-deep gratitude for God's merciful gift of salvation

---

[10] Dante Alighieri, *The Divine Comedy: The Inferno* 3.9.

(Rom. 12:1-2), (3) display the new life of God we have received (Rom. 6:1-4), and (4) result in eternal rewards from God (1 Cor. 3:5-15). But, eternal life is God's *free gift* to the believing sinner.

As Romans 6:23 says, "For the wages of sin is death, but the free gift of God is eternal life in Christ Jesus, our Lord." To say that salvation can be lost through sinful works after we are saved not only misunderstands the character of the life God imparts—it is eternal—but also misunderstands the nature of Christ's work on the cross. Did not our suffering Savior cry out before He died, "It is finished!"? He paid in full the sin debt we owed God and offers eternal salvation, at no cost to us (Jn. 19:30). It is commonly said that "He paid a debt He did not owe because we owed a debt we could not pay." Note the following illustration of the bad news and the glorious good news of Romans 6:23.

Adapted from Bridge to Life © 1969, The Navigators.
Used by permission of The Navigators. All rights reserved.

When do we receive eternal life?

At the very moment we believe! "Whoever believes in Him should not perish, but *has* eternal life." What tense is the verb "has?" Present tense, right? What tense is the verb "believes?" Again, present tense.

The moment you believe in Jesus as God and the only Savior is the same moment His eternal life is imparted to you. This means you have absolute assurance of eternal life from the moment you trust in Jesus as your Savior. From God's viewpoint, you are, from that moment, forever sealed as His very own possession (Eph. 1:13-14). So Paul wrote, "For I am convinced that neither death, nor life, nor angels, nor principalities, nor things present, nor things to come, nor powers, nor height, nor depth, nor any other created thing, will be able to separate us from the love of God, which is in Christ Jesus our Lord" (Rom. 8:38-39). Our joy is uncontained when we ponder the reality of assurance of eternal life based upon God's unchangeable promise. The hymn, "Blessed Assurance" reveals such unbridled joy:

> Blessed assurance, Jesus is mine!
> Oh, what a foretaste of glory divine!
> Heir of salvation, purchase of God,
> Born of His Spirit, washed in His blood.
>
> This is my story, this is my song,
> praising my Savior all the day long.[11]

When you know, without a doubt, that *whatever* happens this side of Heaven, you still have Jesus, praising Him is the natural celebration of your heart!

What exactly is eternal life?

The word "life" is a form of the Greek term "*zoe.*" John often uses this word to describe life as God himself has it. Possessing eternal life is nothing less than the very life of God Himself pulsating in the spiritual veins of a Christian. The reason the Gospel of Jesus Christ is Good News is because God gives the gift of His glorious Self to whoever trusts in Jesus as God-in-flesh and the only Savior. Eternal life is the best gift because it is the gift of God Himself, and God is the Best there is. God is the complete opposite of "boring." In fact, until you trust in Christ as your Savior, you are not really living, but merely existing, filled with nothing but emptiness. The only song you can sing is, "*I can't get no satisfaction.*"[12] You can try, and try, and try, and still the God-shaped vacuum in your soul will remain until you let God Himself fill it. You were made for Him, just as a fish was made for water.

This being true, the very life of God in the believer connects him with God in an endless, personal relationship; after all, it is His eternal Life we receive when we believe! This all-satisfying new relationship with our Creator seems far too good to be true!

Worship the Lord as you ponder the following twenty-six realities (**A** to **Z**) which reveal some of what it means to possess the eternal life of God:

Adopted by God (Rom. 8:15), **B**lessed by God with every spiritual blessing in Christ (Eph. 1:3), a **C**hild of God (Jn. 1:12), **D**ead to sin's ruling power (Rom. 6:11), **E**ternal comfort (2 Thess. 2:16), **F**orgiven of all sins (Eph. 1:7), **G**ifted to serve God (1 Pet. 4:10), **H**ope (Eph. 1:12), **I**ndwelt by the Holy Spirit (Rom. 8:9), **J**ustified (Rom. 3:24), **K**nown by God (2 Tim. 2:19), **L**oved by God (Rom. 8:37-39), **M**ade righteous

---

[11] Fanny J. Crosby, "Blessed Assurance," Hymnary.org, http://www.hymnary.org /text/blessed_assurance_jesus_is_mine.

[12] Rolling Stones, "(I Can't Get No) Satisfaction," Warner/Chappell Music, 1971.

before God (Rom. 5:19), **N**ame written in the Book of Life (Phil. 4:3), **O**ld self crucified (Rom. 6:6), [13] **P**eace with God (Rom. 5:1), **Q**uickened (made alive spiritually) by God (Eph. 2:5), **R**econciled to God (Rom. 5:10), **S**ealed by the Holy Spirit (Eph. 1:13-14), **T**asted the good Word of God (Heb. 6:5), **U**nder God's grace (Rom. 6:14), **V**ictor over the world (1 Jn. 4:4), **W**ashed of all sins (1 Cor. 6:11), e**X**tricated from Hell (Jn. 3:16), **Y**ielding to God commanded and made possible (Rom. 6:12-13), and, **Z**eal for good works commanded and made possible (Tit. 3:4-8).

How does this eternal Life show itself?

Since it is the gift of God Himself indwelling the believer, it shows up in God-like actions, attitudes and words. It is the love, joy, peace, patience, kindness, goodness, gentleness, faithfulness, and self-control that God Himself possesses. His Beautiful Life will be seen in the believer who allows himself to be controlled by the Holy Spirit who indwells him (Gal. 5:22-23; Eph. 5:18-20). This God-glorifying behavior is called the "fruit of repentance," in Matthew 3:8, where John the Baptist commanded, "bear fruit in keeping with repentance."

According to Luke, "The crowds then asked him, 'What shall we do?' And he would answer and say to them, 'The man who has two tunics is to share with him who has none; and he who has food is to do likewise.' And *some* tax collectors also came to be baptized, and they said to him, 'Teacher, what shall we do?' And he said to them, 'Collect no more than what you have been ordered to.' *Some* soldiers were questioning him, saying, 'And *what about* us, what shall we do?' And he said to them, 'Do not take money from anyone by force, or accuse *anyone* falsely, and be content with your wages'" (3:10-14).

Once a person changes his mind from *not* trusting in Jesus for eternal life *to* trusting in Jesus for eternal life, God commands him to bear outward fruit of inward repentance.[14] "Therefore, brothers, by the mercies of God, I urge you to present your bodies as a living sacrifice, holy and pleasing to God; this is your spiritual worship. Do not be conformed to this age, but be transformed by the renewing of your mind, so that you may discern what is the good, pleasing, and perfect will of God" (Rom. 12:1-2).

To summarize the truth that God cannot offer us a better deal than trusting in Jesus for eternal life, an old parable says, "A silly servant who is

---

[13] Refers to our former spiritual identity before God as an unsaved person. That identity no longer exists. Our old self died.

[14] Repentance looks at the change in one's belief, while the fruits of repentance look at the change in one's behavior. Repentance concerns justification while the fruits of repentance concern sanctification.

told to open the door sets his shoulder to it and pushes with all his might, but the door stirs not, and he cannot enter, use what strength he may. Another comes with a key and easily unlocks the door and enters right readily."[15]

Those who would be saved by works are pushing at Heaven's gate without result, but faith is the key that opens the gate at once. God cannot offer us a better deal than His invitation to put our faith in the crucified and risen Lord Jesus to forgive our sins and receive His eternal life as a free gift.

[15] Michael Green, ed., *1500 Illustrations for Biblical Preaching* (Grand Rapids: Baker, 1989), 319.

5

CONCLUSION

John 3:16 reveals that God finds it impossible to love us with a greater love, He finds it impossible to give us a greater gift, and He finds it impossible to offer us a better deal. What a Love. What a Gift. What an Offer. *What a Savior is Jesus Christ, the Lord!*

> O for a thousand tongues to sing
> My great Redeemer's praise,
> The glories of my God and King,
> The triumphs of His grace.[16]

Your response

If you have never trusted in Jesus alone for eternal Life, why not now? Be born again, spiritually. Escape the endless torment of Hell and embrace Jesus Christ and endless Joy. Right now, "Believe (trust) in the Lord Jesus, and you shall be saved" (Acts 16:31).

You may wish to express your trust in Jesus in prayer: *"Dear God, I admit that I need Your forgiveness and deserve eternal punishment for my sins. I believe that Jesus is God in a body and that His death offers forgiveness for my sins and His resurrection offers Your free gift of eternal Life. I now put my trust in Jesus alone as my Savior. Thank you for saving me. I rejoice that I am forever Your child!"*

---

[16] Charles Wesley, "O for a Thousand Tongues to Sing My Dear Redeemer's Praise," Hymnary.org, 1739, http://www.hymnary.org/text/o_for_a_thousand _tongues_to_sing_my.

Once you trust in Jesus as your Savior, the following will help you *grow into a strong Christian*:

- Write the date you trusted Jesus as Savior in your Bible, and write John 3:16 next to the date. When you doubt that you now have eternal Life, go back to John 3:16, and quote it out loud—several times if necessary—to resist any demon that may be on the attack (Gen. 3:1-6; 2 Cor. 11:3; Eph. 6:10-18). *Rejoice* in the assurance of your eternal salvation (I Jn. 5:11-13).

- Begin following Jesus daily as your Master (Lk. 9:23; Rom. 12:1-2), obeying His commands by the power of the Holy Spirit (Eph. 5:18-21).

- Tell others (e.g., friends and family) that you have trusted in Jesus as your Savior (Jn. 4:39-42).

- Start reading the New Testament, several chapters a day; over the next year, or two, read the entire Bible.

- Talk to God throughout the day. He is your Heavenly Father (Matt. 6:9-13). Bring your needs and requests to Him, and He will replace your worries with His peace (Phil. 4:6-7).

- Write out Bible verses on 3x5 cards (or whatever you can carry with you) and memorize a verse of Scripture each week, then review what you memorize. You can begin by choosing the verses in this booklet. Hide God's Word in your heart. Treasure Him more than your necessary food (Ps. 119:9-11; Job 23:12).

- Now that God dwells within you (1 Cor. 6:18-20), with His power, you can turn away from sin (Rom. 8:13; 1Cor. 10:12-14). If you give into temptation, confess your sins to God and He will forgive you and restore your fellowship with Him (1 Jn. 1:7-9). *You have not lost your salvation when you sin*, but your fellowship with God has been broken (Ps. 32).

- Find a church that teaches the Bible, shares Christ with lost people, loves one another and is willing to help you grow into a strong Christian (Acts 2:41-47). Talk to the pastor about your need to be baptized, in obedience to Christ, as you publicly identify yourself as one of His followers (Matt. 28:18-20; Acts 16:30-34).

- Worship and adore the Lord Jesus Christ! Each day meditate on passages about the Cross (examples: Ps. 22; Isa. 53; Matt. 27; Mk. 15; Lk. 23; Jn. 19); ask God to make you a Cross-Centered Christian. Remembering what He suffered to deliver us from eternal suffering is crucial to staying in love with Him (Eph. 6:24; Rev. 2:4).

- Share the gospel with unsaved people, just as Jesus shares with Nicodemus in John 3. Jonathan Edwards resolved to *live each day as if*

17

he'd already seen the horror of Hell and the happiness of Heaven.[17] Ask God to help you see lost people through His eyes of compassion (Matt. 9:35-38). And ask Him for courage (Acts 4:29-31).

- Pray for the salvation of lost friends, family, relatives, co-workers, and neighbors. As you pray, ask God to use you to bring many lost people to the nail-scarred hands of the crucified and risen Jesus. God desires all people to be saved (1Tim. 2:4; 2 Pet. 3:9), though He knows that not all will be. Knowing this will help you see lost people as He does, and develop the same desire for their salvation as He does. *Your motivation to share the gospel and pray for lost people will be fueled by His desires becoming your desires,* a truth modeled by Paul (Rom. 9:1-3; 10:1).

Simply put, *savor the Savior, and you will share the Savior.* As you walk with Him, day by day, reading His Word and conversing with Him in prayer, you will find that *He is far too wonderful* to keep to yourself! May God bless you and use you to take many to Heaven with you.

Some want to live within the sound of church or chapel bell; I want to run a rescue shop within a yard of Hell.

– C.T. Studd

---

[17] Jonathan Edwards, Sereno Edwards Dwight, and Edward Hickman. *The Works of Jonathan Edwards* (London: W. Ball, 1839), 1:lxiv.

QUESTIONS FOR PERSONAL OR GROUP STUDY

1. What is the context of John 3:16?
2. What does Nicodemus need to know?
3. What is the first thing God finds impossible to do?
4. What is the role of the word "so" in John 3:16?
5. What is the first mannerism of God's love in verse 16?
6. What is the second mannerism?
7. Who is "the world," in this context?
8. As inhabitants of this world, what are we like?
9. According to Romans 5:8, what is God's attitude toward us, even though we are His enemies?
10. What is our natural disposition before God as those born with a sin nature?
11. What is a third mannerism of God's love in John 3:16?
12. What is the meaning and importance of the word "whoever"?
13. What is the second thing God finds impossible to do?
14. To be the greatest gift of all, why did Jesus have to be fully God?
15. To be the greatest gift of all, why did Jesus have to be fully man?
16. What does the word "begotten" mean, as applied to Jesus in John 3:16?
17. What does the word "Son" mean, as applied to Jesus in John 3:16?
18. Why was Jesus crucified, according to John 10:31-39?
19. Since Jesus never denied His claim to be equal with God, He was either a L____, a L____, or He is L_____ of Lords.
20. When you read the details of the crucifixion, how does it affect you?
21. What is the third thing God finds impossible to do?
22. What is the condition for possessing eternal life in John 3:16?
23. What does the word "believe" mean?

24. What is involved in repentance?
25. What is not involved in repentance? (see footnote 8)
26. Complete the statement: "Repentance and turning to God are wrapped up in b_____ (trusting) in His Son, Jesus, for e_____ L____."
27. "Asking Jesus into our heart" is a common expression in churches and gospel tracts. How should we think about this concept? (see footnote 9)
28. What does it mean (and *not* mean) to "perish" in John 3:16?
29. List 5 things an unbeliever experiences after he dies (per Luke 16:19-31).
30. How should our understanding of the doctrine of Hell affect our outreach to lost people?
31. Why is the punishment of the unsaved so severe?
32. According to John 3:16, what is the basis for saying that once a person is saved, he is always saved?
33. When does a person receive eternal life?
34. What is the basis for assurance of salvation?
35. What is eternal life?
36. Why is eternal life the best gift of all?
37. How does eternal life show itself in the believer?
38. What is the difference between "repentance" and the "fruits of repentance"?
39. Do you believe that Jesus is God and have you placed your trust in Him alone as your Savior?
40. Spend 30 minutes thanking God for (1) Jesus Christ (review *A to Z* section on who Jesus is), (2) what He has saved you from (review Luke 16:19-31), and (3) what He has given you as a recipient of His eternal life (review *A to Z* section under "*What exactly is eternal life?*")
41. Complete the statement: "Simply put, s_____ the S_____ and you will s_____ the S_____."
42. Do you find yourself sharing the Savior with lost people? Why? Why not?
43. List the names of *5 lost people* (e.g., neighbors, co-workers, family, relatives, hair stylist, friends at the gym, etc.) for whom you will begin praying and fasting and with whom you will share the *good news of Jesus*!

BIBLIOGRAPHY

Edwards, Jonathan, Sereno Edwards Dwight, and Edward Hickman. *The Works of Jonathan Edwards*. 2 Vols. London: W. Ball, 1839.

Foster, Elon. *New Cyclopedia of Illustrations: Adapted to Christian Teaching: Embracing Mythology, Analogies Legends, Parables, Emblems, Metaphors, Similes, Allegories, Proverbs; Classic, Historic, and Religious Anecdotes, etc.* New York: W. C. Palmer, 1870.

Green, Michael, ed. *1500 Illustrations for Biblical Preaching*. Grand Rapids: Baker, 1989.

Larson, Craig Brian, ed. *Illustrations for Preaching & Teaching: From Leadership Journal*. Grand Rapids: Baker, 1993.

Yancey, Philip. *What's so Amazing About Grace?* Grand Rapids: Zondervan, 1997.

ABOUT THE AUTHOR

Ron Barnes is the Teaching Pastor of Casa de Oro Baptist Church in Spring Valley, California. He is also a Professor of Biblical Studies at Southern California Seminary (socalsem.edu). Ron and his wife, Ginny, have 3 grown daughters, and 9 grandchildren. You can listen to the podcasts of Dr. Barnes' sermons at www.cdobaptist.com.

JOHN 3:16

"For God so loved the world that He gave His only begotten Son, that whoever believes in Him should not perish, but have eternal life."

www.ingramcontent.com/pod-product-compliance
Lightning Source LLC
Chambersburg PA
CBHW060605030426
42337CB00019B/3614